WATERMEAD PATHWAYS
Reflections and Memories

ChristGift

Fr John Daley IC

Watermead Publishing Limited

WATERMEAD PATHWAYS
Reflections and Memories
Book Three **"Christgift"**

ISBN 978-1-907721-03-8

© John Daley *(Individual Texts)*

© 2013 Alison Kennedy *("ChristGift" Presentation)*

First Published 5th December 2013 by
Watermead Publishing Limited,
Watermead Centre,
St Joseph's, 12 Goodwood Road,
Leicester LE5 6SG
Telephone 0116 2207881

Cover Picture from the painting in watercolours
"Monte Calvario" by Matthew Concannon

Additional illustrations by
Sheila Jackson, Alison Kennedy, David Kennedy
and Watermead's *"Little Saints"* © AMK

Editing, design, and typesetting by Alison Kennedy
with a thank you to Mary Fortey for typing up the original texts
and to Doreen Concannon, our proof reader.

Watermead Publishing Apostolate
www.watermead-apostolate.com

Printed by AnchorPrint, Syston, Leicestershire
www.anchorprint.co.uk

Watermead Pathways Series
Book One *"FaithGift"* published April 2010
Book Two *"LoveGift"* published March 2011

Other Publications from the Watermead Apostolate
"Words of Prayer and Encouragement" (published by Watermead Publishing Ltd)
"Words of Prayer and Reflection" (published by Catholic Printing Company of Farnworth)
"Voices of the Gospels" by Colleen Wethered (published by Catholic Printing Company of Farnworth)
"Tom, an English Irishman" by T.P. Concannon (published by Watermead Publishing Ltd)
"O Lord, Hear my Prayer" (published by Watermead Publishing Ltd)
"Getting to Know the Bible" (published by Redemptorist Publications)

Contents

"Christmas at the edge of Canadian wilderness.
Joy shared with families, friends, frontier apostles
and our inspiring Bishop Fergus O'Grady.
Fr John Brioux's evocative drawing
touches rich memories for us"

CHRISTMAS CARD

Since I was a little boy I have had a favourite type of Christmas Card. It is a snow scene, and there is a church.

Many are the variations of the scene. Sometimes a few houses, sometimes people on their way to or from church, sometimes only the church. Why does the scene hold me?

Possibly I am associating the joy of Christmas Day and worship at the church as part of our family celebration with this scene. But we did not live in the countryside. We were city. Our church was surrounded by blocks of streets. There were no trees, no fields. I don't remember snow. Snow came later, in January.

It was imagination. The Christmas card scene I had never seen. I still haven't. Trees don't hold snow as pictured on Christmas cards. No matter how heavy a fall of snow we still see plenty of the bare brown branches or of the evergreen foliage. Christmas card trees are all white.

So, my favourite Christmas card is of a picture that never was. Yet it causes me to tingle. It is not beautiful or touching as the manger scene is - child, Mary and Joseph - but it sets up associations which take me back to a time when I knew faith only through the love of my family.

Years had to pass before I could think of faith in God as my own and not simply as part of a lovely home and family.

That Christmas card is home, then. It appealed to my childish imagination by its countryside setting and beauty, and belonged to a lovely time of the year when it was cosy to be in the house and we thought of family and friends and bought each other presents.

And the church? It gave meaning to the beauty of the scene. What we celebrated in church was the meaning of Christmas, I knew. But imagination and association held powerful messages for me - even more than the reality of the baby in the manger.

Is that unusual? People prefer watching Coronation Street to knowing real neighbours. Prefer watching `Neighbours' to being out. Hate hospitals but weep comfortably at a film. Like a good romance, but find married life dull. Enjoy gossip and scandal, which require no thought, but find real news of world and national and local importance boring because that requires effort to understand.

When I was a child, I thought as a child. Now I am a man I must learn to see things as they are. Imagination is a beautiful gift. It is not an escape from reality.

"When I was a child, I talked like a child,
I thought like a child, I reasoned like a child.
When I became a man,
I put the ways of childhood behind me."

1 Corinthians 13:10 -11

OUR SCHOOL NATIVITY

Our school Nativity play has been well rehearsed and I shall enjoy the children's toothless smiles and grins, their waves at their families, forgotten lines and sudden nerves, and watching reality break into the stage story. Every year it's the same event!

The birth of Jesus will be celebrated in a sentimental glow of children's supposed innocence and with a vague nod in the direction of God for granting us the Incarnation. The simple crib is beautiful – the babe, Mary and Joseph – but a crowded school stage isn't teaching a simple story, it is aiming at pleasing parents and avoiding criticism.

I love the Christmas stories – but there are two: one told by St. Luke and one by St. Matthew. They are so different from each other that the only common details are a birth at Bethlehem and the names of Jesus, Mary and Joseph. All other details are different, and I find it difficult to like the school Nativity play that lumps the two stories together as though they were one and adds all possible combinations of characters in order to find places for the children.

St. Luke tells of Mary and Joseph living in Nazareth, journeying to Bethlehem for a census that history does not know and for a reason that the Roman Empire never used – for everyone to go home to be registered. That would be madness. No Roman occupation would risk confusion and opportunity for uprising just to count its population. No Roman census made that condition. St. Luke has something else in mind.

There would be no need for Mary to travel, so why does Joseph bring her on a difficult five-day journey when she is heavily pregnant. That is either cruel or foolish. What does the Gospel mean? Bethlehem is called Joseph's home-town, therefore his relatives are there. What Jewish family would allow a young girl to have her first child in a stable? "No room at the inn" is a symbolic truth, not a real story, as we slowly realise all of St. Luke's beautifully crafted narrative is. The shepherds are the Old Testament chosen leaders who longed for the fulfilling of God's promises – Abraham, Isaac, Jacob, Moses, David – all shepherds chosen by God. The Old Testament comes to the crib to honour the Messiah for whom they had longed.

St. Matthew tells the story very differently. Mary and Joseph live in Bethlehem and Jesus is born in their home. The Magi enter their dwelling place to honour the child with mystical gifts: gold for a king, frankincense for a god, and myrrh for a saviour. Matthew's story is full of symbolism, also. The journey of the Magi is a reflection of Isaiah's vision of the whole world coming on pilgrimage to acknowledge God, guided by the star of wisdom. The world, represented by the Magi, acknowledges the babe as King, God and Saviour.

I love the Christmas stories in Matthew and Luke, the reflection of the world and Israel coming to Bethlehem to acknowledge the Messiah and Saviour born for them, but I am uncomfortable with the sentimentality in parent-pleasing school Nativity plays.

"Baby born at Bethlehem
Mother and baby doing well!"

THE THREE GIFTS

Marcus was fifteen. His local school organised community visits around the area and Marcus was one of the volunteers visiting the elderly and the housebound. His particular care was Nora, lovely elderly lady living about a mile from his home.

On Christmas Day his family gathered, as usual, for the celebrations. At dinner he told his Grandma how much he would like to call to see Nora that afternoon, just to wish her a happy Christmas.

"Grandpa will take you," she said, "you ask him."

"I'd love to give her a present," said Marcus, "but I have nothing to give her out of my presents, they wouldn't suit her!"

He thought. "Grandma" he said, "I have a ten pound note. Could I put that inside her card as my present?"

"She won't want a present," said Grandma, "she will just be glad you wanted to see her. But if you want to give it to her, you do. She will be pleased."

Grandpa and Marcus went to visit Nora and she was delighted to see them. Marcus gave her the card and said there was a little present inside it for her. She smiled and thanked him.

They stayed for a cup of tea, and then got up to go. "And now," said Nora, "I have a card for you!" She brought it, and added "and inside there is a little gift for you." She smiled.

When they got home Marcus opened the card. Inside was a £10 note. It was his Christmas present from Nora! Marcus was fifteen, just too young to know what Grandma and Grandpa knew - it was the same £10 note.

On Christmas day a £10 note became three gifts, and each of them precious.

ST MATTHEW'S CHRISTMAS STORY

"This is how Jesus Christ came to be born." . . . So opens the painful nativity story in St. Matthew's Gospel. Joseph's anguish is very moving. He and Mary are betrothed, implying a promise of the home and family they would share – a situation we all know well, full of hope and expectancy, of love and trust, of family encouragement and joy.

When Mary discovers she is with child by the Holy Spirit there is no dilemma about the conception: she is with child by the Holy Spirit – she knows and Joseph knows. God has acted: the engagement is shattered and normal home and family expectations fade into a sad memory: God has chosen Mary and he, Joseph, must move aside. The loneliness is desperate. He shares Mary's secret and can tell no one. His love for her has been usurped by a wonder he cannot understand – she is with child by the Holy Spirit.

He must go, but where? He must leave Mary to God, but how? Joseph's anguish guides him. He knows her innocence and now sees her goodness and beauty in a new way because he glimpses what God has seen – but he must make a decision, alone.

If he divorces Mary according to the Law she will be declared to be with child, guilty of adultery, and thus condemned to be stoned to death. He, Joseph, would have to throw the first stone – but he knows she is innocent.

If he deserts her by casually walking away, "divorcing her informally", (he has the right in law to do that) he will be condemned by all for deserting his betrothed and leaving her with child. He will have to pay compensation as demanded by the Law, but he is free to leave her. Matthew tells us that this was Joseph's decision – to divorce Mary informally.

Then, and only then, God steps into the story through a message from an unnamed angel. Joseph is not to fear taking Mary as his wife because she is with child by the Holy Spirit: he is to marry her and name the child as his own. Joseph obeys, but it is not the home and family he had planned. The will of God is clear and Joseph has been invited to share Mary's blessing.

The pain and sadness of the story continue. Strange stories, rich in symbolism, of wise men mistakenly coming to Jerusalem; Herod's cruelty in killing baby boys in Bethlehem; Joseph and Mary fleeing home to go down into Egypt – are full of memories of another Joseph and his saving Jacob and his brothers by bringing them down into Egypt. Israel's and Judah's exiles to Assyria and Babylon are recalled in Rachel's weeping for her children, as she weeps for Bethlehem now. Then, when the tyrant is dead and Joseph knows he can return to the Promised Land (another memory – of Moses and Joshua) he does not return home to Bethlehem but goes instead to Galilee to begin a new life in Nazareth.

The wonder of the birth of Jesus is set in a story full of pain and sadness, rich with biblical, historical and symbolic references; the Old Testament finds fulfilment in the New. St. Joseph is the hapless bearer of great pain with not a single note of joy in Matthew's account (yet there is much joy in Luke's account). "Fear" is the last emotion of Joseph that we read of before he and Mary settle into the silent mystery of their virginal marriage in Nazareth.

COME AND SEE
    THE CAUSE WHY THINGS
        THUS FRAGRANT BE

          THE DARLING
            OF THE WORLD
              IS COME

          AND FIT IT IS
           WE FIND A ROOM
        TO WELCOME HIM.

     AWAKE THE VOICE!
    AWAKE THE STRING!
   HEART, EAR. AND EYE
AND EVERYTHING.   Robert Herrick 1591~1674

A CHRISTMAS STORY

The couple came to see me one evening early in December. I did not know them, nor their problem - they had simply asked to come. They told me their sad story.

The young woman had come to the town in September, to attend college, leaving him, a little older than she was, working in their home town and beginning to save for their future. They had hoped to marry, though were not yet actually engaged.

After a few weeks into the new term she had been invited to a party, along with several other girls who were also new. There were not many at the party and the drinks were drugged. She remembered waking up feeling heavy and sick, and walking to her digs in a daze.

When her period was late, she became afraid. On discovering she was with child she realised it must have been that night. Someone had taken advantage of her.

She told her boyfriend and he had come. Of course he believed her - he knew and loved her. But he was bewildered and anguished and that is why they had come to see me. They wanted to talk to someone before going home to their families, where decisions needed to be faced.

She was clear. This was her child, only hers. She did not know the father, nor did she want to. The child was hers, and she wanted the boyfriend to receive the child from her so that it would be his, and he be the father.

He understood. But there was his agony. He did not know if he could accept the responsibility. He was afraid that every time he looked at the child he would feel hatred for the man who had touched his girl, and, because he could not hate him directly, he might hate the child instead. The girl tried to reassure him, as she must have done numerous times already. There was no father. The child was hers. He would be the father.

I was held in the horror of the pain they knew. She, the mother, had adjusted: the child was there and would be loved - she had become

8

woman. But he was still the warrior, not yet man. He wanted to smash and to hate the one who had caused it all: to blame and punish. He was not yet ready to heal or be healed.

I asked if they had considered abortion (I needed to know their moral stand). They had considered, but only to firmly reject it. "He is a Catholic," she said, simply, as though being Catholic gave the answer, "and I know abortion is wrong. This is a child."

I was glad. If the baby were to live without threat, then God was here. We could start from the promise of the baby's life.

It was the Christmas story. The maiden was with child and the betrothed in agony. I, being no angel, tried to say it. No, said the young man. The Christmas story was beautiful because God had chosen Mary; but their story was ugly because a dirty student had used his girl. I understood his contrast, but saw two lovely women waiting quietly for decision.

We talked till late. When they went I watched them as far as the corner, and waved. I closed the door of the safe little presbytery from the cold of the night, and my anger seethed. Somewhere in our town was scum, knowing and caring nothing of this evening. For a laugh he and his mates had drugged the girls they had invited to a party, and then taken their choice. He would never know he had chosen a ready womb.

His Christmas would probably be drink, and lots of it. Drunken shouts of "Merry Christmas" around the pubs, with other chicks in sight, and mates just like himself. Imagine wishing him a Happy Christmas.

And what would be Christmas for the young couple, in the sadness of a new life thrust upon them? Her studies were over, and she would not be returning to the town. The families back home would share the grief and pain of their two children. Christmas would be quiet and sad - maybe the shadow would always be there.

So simple a moment at a party. So explosive its consequences.

In the following March I received a letter from the young woman. She said that her boyfriend had finally told her that he would never be able to accept the child. What to do next was her choice - he had left it to her. Poor girl. Like the student who had taken her, he was to be yet another not a man. He had said he loved her, yet, at this most difficult moment of her life, he left her alone to decide.

What was her choice? Live alone with her child, give the child for adoption, choose between her boyfriend and her baby.

She had had an abortion, she wrote, and she felt that she was now in hell, knowing she had chosen her baby to die.

I have heard nothing since. I know God holds them all somewhere in his love - the baby with him, the girl in gentle forgiveness and the boy in sad disappointment that he did not love as he thought he did. Then, there's the student - a family man now, probably.

Song of Life

O Child, you are from God and he loves you eternally;
He formed you in the womb, you're the gift of His love.
In the springtime of your life you will grow and laugh and play:
May the peace of Christ be yours
through the love of each day.

The years will follow on from springtime to summertime;
your world can bloom with joy in the light of God's love.
You will glorify the Lord when you walk along His way:
May the peace of Christ be yours
through the love of each day.

God's favour rest with you through the years of your autumn time;
leaves red and brown and gold tell the tale of your days.
And the wisdom of the Lord be in all you do and say:
May the peace of Christ be yours
through the love of each day.

Fear not the darkened skies when you come to the winter time;
Jesus' birth at Bethlehem is the promise of spring.
All the ages hear His word that the Easter day will come
when the peace of Christ is ours,
joy eternal our home.

CHILD IN THE WOMB

I was invited to speak on local radio. I chose as the theme "reverence for life" and submitted the following as one of my scripts:

"The nurse came to see me. She worked at the local hospital on the maternity and gynaecology wards. She was a Catholic, but had long given up the practice of her faith. She felt no qualms about any of the work that her duties called upon her to do, and she had accepted that she would take her turn on rota when it came to abortion. She had seen a number of women for whom termination seemed to be the right answer, and she was willing to help.

A few days previously, she told me, she had been assisting at an abortion. As the child came out of the womb it gave a cry. "Get rid of the thing," said the surgeon, and gave her the tiny body of the baby she had just heard cry.

She had to get rid of it, into the pail that would later be taken to the incinerator.

She felt sick. When her shift was over she went to the relevant hospital authority and said she would not again work on an abortion. She was understood and was promised she would be given other duties. Her job was safe. "Now," she said, "I'm thinking about God again. I saw Him because of that baby's cry."

The station refused to allow this to be broadcast, saying that listeners would be upset. I admitted the incident was upsetting - that was the point of the talk; but it was also inspiring - a nurse had found God through the cry of an aborted baby.

I puzzled the refusal. The baby's cry, the incinerator, the nurse's turning to God, the implication that every aborted child cried out within the womb, the faith that a child died and was not destroyed, and was now with God ... Were these the reasons? None had been given.

A child dies. That's what the talk was asserting. No one was being judged or condemned. With fourteen years of hospital chaplaincy as my experience I would be careful not to condemn. I had seen terminations and abortions close to, for too long and too often, to judge anyone. From convenient abortion (the woman having her fourth in five years, refusing to be sterilised in case she should one day want a child) to agonising termination (the woman begging to go to the limits of her strength to give the child the chance to be born, but accepting the sympathetic surgeon's judgment that it had now become impossible), I had shared the bewilderment and pain and matter-of-factness of patients and staff. I have sat in on nurse-training conferences and heard of the students' startled reaction to lecturers who had told them to cite abortion as a means of birth control in their exams, and had senior staff sneer at me that Catholic women were as ready for abortion as any other - what good did I think I could do?

Be available, I had supposed. Help, if I could. Pray, as I might - even offer to pray at the incinerator (Church permission refused). And always the longing to share the faith that the child in the womb is God's child.

How willingly women who had miscarriages accepted that the lost child was with God. Equally openly, women who had suffered abortions came to acknowledge their child had died, not been destroyed, and they would know each other in eternal life. How beautifully the women spoke of such understanding, changing a grief of loss into a grief of love.

"I saw my child," said one, the day after her miscarriage, "and she was beautiful".

"They let you see her!" I was startled.

"I begged to," she smiled, "and I know God would not have given me someone so beautiful to simply lose her. She is with Him. Clare was the name waiting for her. She is a saint now, and I have been praying to her all night."

I felt privileged to hear such love and faith. I spoke of it at mass, and a priest called it "sentimental punk" but did not explain why. Limbo, perhaps.

With the Church, I long to speak for the child in the womb and God's love. The radio refused. Was the talk intemperate from an unknown? Would well-known Catholic speakers be more free, or would they also be refused, told to keep to safe subjects? Have they been?

One priest told me I was a fool to choose such a sensitive topic. Radio and listeners were not ready for challenge of abortion, and I was missing an opportunity to give something of the Christian message in a safer way. (A priest friend in South Africa spoke against the injustice of apartheid and was threatened with expulsion. His brethren urged him to be quiet, do the good the Government left them free to do ...) Was there imbalance in my talk?

I decided to share my disappointment in our local ecumenical magazines. The editor of one refused to publish it, objecting that it would upset people who had decided in good conscience to have an abortion. Isaiah, Jeremiah, the Book of Psalms, all witness to the love of God for the child in the womb, I said. That's what I wanted to say, and to share the joy of the nurse who had found God by recognising a child in the womb. Wasn't that a human and Christian message?

Frank Lake, "A Doctor's Response to a Healing Pope", quotes an angry journalist at one of his conferences urging the women present to reject his views on the personal life of the foetus. "Did they not have the intelligence to see that if a woman got to think of the thing in their wombs as a person - with a real personal life of its own - aborting it would become emotionally impossible."

The child in the womb cannot speak, but it cries out within the womb. Its cry is a plea for life on behalf of all the unborn, and those who hear the truth of that cry should speak.

Then the cry from the womb, which many women know and that nurse heard, will be heard by all.

"I knew you
before I formed you in your mother's womb.
Before you were born I set you apart
and appointed you as my prophet to the nations."

Jeremiah 1:5

CHRISTMAS AT 40 BELOW

Look at the map of Canada. Go to the south-west coast line and travel north from the city of Vancouver. Travelling up that coast line for about five hundred miles (two or three inches to you), you will come to the little port of Prince Rupert. Follow the road inland from Prince Rupert. It rises to Terrace and Hazelton for about a hundred and twenty miles and then slopes to the south east, running towards the Canadian Rockies. Along that road you will come to Prince George. That's where I was, Christmas Day, 1971, saying Mass in a little wooden chapel, and the temperature outside was 40 below zero.

I had arrived in the September. Beautiful autumn days, when the school term opened and I was teaching at Prince George College. But as we moved into October, the temperature began falling and wasn't going to stop. When I commented on the cold, the local people laughed. We were still above zero! Wait until we went below and stayed there. Wait until we reached 40 below!

The snow came in the first week of November. It stayed. And more. And the temperature falling. But a brisk, invigorating cold it was, and wrapped up against it, it seemed less uncomfortable than the dampness of our own British winter. How beautiful the constant ice-blue of the skies, and how fascinating the lovely clear night skies when the snow stopped falling and the stillness of the cold air and the surrounding wooded hills were what we could be most aware of.

Towards Christmas, we were in the twenties below zero and people commented that we might reach 40 below before Christmas. Forty degrees below seemed a sort of landmark - reach there, and you could genuinely claim to have been in a Canadian winter. By now, I could not tell the temperature at all. It was always very cold, too cold to walk more than you had to, and always necessary to wrap up when outside - clearing away snow or doing any other odd jobs.

Two friends had been to hospital suffering from mild frost-bite, after clearing snow from their driveways and not wearing anything on their heads and faces. (A favourite head-gear was a woollen balaclava that

14

had only an eye slit: very useful if you had to be out for more than a few minutes.)

In the week before Christmas, we reached the thirties below zero, and still going down.

On Christmas morning, I got up at 6.00 am. I was to say Mass at 9.00, 10.30 and 12.15. Having shaved and showered, I turned on the radio for the seven o'clock news. We had reached 40 below! I could not tell from the warmth of the little cabin where I was living; an oil stove kept the small spaces of sitting-room and bedroom reasonably warm and comfortable always. But I had yet to turn on the heating in the chapel - a small A-framed structure which held about ninety people. The chapel was sixty yards away.

I ran, willing myself not to feel the cold. I genuflected to the Blessed Sacrament and turned on the heating. Two hours hot air blowing would warm the little place by nine o'clock. I walked back briskly, this time wanting to feel the cold of 40 below. And I did. I remember gasping as the cold went into and through me. I was feeling 40 below zero, unprotected by coat or jacket. The relief of the warm cabin again, and the shock of the cold still inside me. It passed. Morning prayer and breakfast, and then over to the chapel again to prepare the altar for Mass.

Christmas greetings to all from all as they arrived. You can't keep quiet on a frosty cold morning, and the children were excited, and everyone knew everyone, so it was a bustling period, leading up to Mass. Wales and home seemed a long, happy way away. I still belonged there. I'd be remembered at the family meals and get-together, but in the meantime I belonged and was happy here, in a little northern mission, celebrating Christmas in the way known to be best . . . thanking God in the sacrifice of the Mass for the wonder of Christ's birth.

ST LUKE'S CHRISTMAS STORY

In chapter 3 of St. Luke's Gospel John the Baptist begins to prepare the way of the Lord in a clear historical setting. The political rulers in Rome and the Holy Land are named, as are the high priests, and we can judge the year to be 27-28 AD. The introduction to Luke's Gospel (written later, as all introductions are) also seems to give a clear political and social setting for the birth of Jesus at Bethlehem – although scholars are puzzled by the details of the story.

A world census at this time does not appear in Roman records. Ten years after Jesus' birth Quirinius was governor of Syria and ordered a local Palestinian census, but that cannot be this Gospel census. Roman history knows of no census which required returning to one's own town to be registered - the logistics of such a condition would be almost impossible and would have served no purpose. Roman rule could not tolerate such mass movement of people with all its opportunity for rebellious unrest. The only reason a man might move home for a census would be to claim family property, lest it be confiscated from the absentee owner.

Possibly, Joseph owned land or property in the Bethlehem region and, to safeguard it, might have decided to go there. But Mary would not need to go. She would have no claim on land. She was with child and would be better staying at home with family and friends to help her at the birth – rather than struggling over a five-day journey through rough terrain and bandit-infested country with its military-patrolled roads.

If Mary and Joseph saw a birth at Bethlehem something beautiful to prepare for (but why – why not Nazareth?) they would have planned carefully. Joseph's relatives would have been in Bethlehem and district, and they would look after a young mother delivering her first child. Jewish family love is proverbial. The family would not reject her, so the reference to an inn is puzzling. The interpretation that Joseph brought a pregnant Mary on a long, unnecessary and painful journey that finishes with rejection is insulting to him and his family.

Rather, we accept that Luke's story is one full of symbolism. When the child is born a host of angels rejoice, witnessed by a group of bewildered and terrified shepherds. The leading angel invites the shepherds to go to Bethlehem to see the new-born baby. The shepherds discover a large crowd of people with Joseph, Mary and the child and tell them what they have heard and seen. Is this crowd of people the family and friends of Joseph?

Then, who are the shepherds? Scripture invites us to discover their names: Abraham, Isaac, Jacob, Moses, David – all shepherds called to look after God's people. The story is a fulfilment of a Messianic longing and the "shepherds" symbolise the leaders of God's people in their long wait for the coming of the Messiah. The shepherds of the Old Testament were patriarchs, prophets and kings – and we "see them" in Luke's story trying to share their faith in the Messiah with the people.

The Holy Family stayed some weeks in Bethlehem, until after the Presentation in the Temple, before returning home to Nazareth (Luke 2:19). Where did they stay? Not in a stable, surely. The story of the coming of the wise men in St. Matthew's Gospel seems to suggest the family had a home in Bethlehem as well as, later, in Nazareth.

The birth of Jesus is not a simple story and the two accounts in Luke and Matthew have in common only the names of the Holy Family and a birth at Bethlehem. All other details are either in the one Gospel or the other. It is clear that the Evangelists wrote with entirely different intentions. We pray to read and understand what the two stories are revealing to us of God's love and the birth of our Saviour.

THE VISITATION

Mary's journey to visit Elizabeth after the Annunciation by the Angel Gabriel seems unnecessary and even pointless: why would she undertake that five or six day walk?

Elizabeth would not have needed Mary to assist her. Zechariah, her husband, was a priest and they would have been surrounded by the other priestly families to care for her during her pregnancy and childbirth.

Would Mary have been able to tell her family of the Angel Gabriel's revelation that Elizabeth was with child? No one would have believed her.

And the roads of the Roman-occupied Holy Land were patrolled by Roman soldiers and passed through bandit-infested country. Would Joseph have allowed Mary, his betrothed, to go on such a dangerous unnecessary journey?

The meaning of "The Visitation" should not be reduced to a kind cousinly gesture: it is a powerful symbolic story of the longing for motherhood in the Old Testament (Sarah, Rachel, Hannah all waited many years for a child) being felt once more in Elizabeth. The longing of these women is an image the longing of Israel for the Messiah, and the child in Mary's womb is fulfilling that longing. The Visitation becomes the completion of the Old Testament in Elizabeth and John, the beginning of the New Testament in Mary and Jesus.

In Mary and Elizabeth the two Testaments meet. John, in the womb of Elizabeth, is the final prophet of the Old Testament – the one to prepare the way for the Lord, to make his paths straight. Jesus, in the womb of Mary, is the fulfilment of the longing of Israel for the coming of the Messiah, the Saviour. The two women sing the wonderful "Magnificat" – "My soul glorifies the Lord . . ."

Some ancient manuscripts have Elizabeth singing the Magnificat, and indeed it reflects her joy as beautifully as it does Mary's: but as the hymn progresses we hear a third voice – of the people of Israel, the Woman Israel, rejoicing in God's favour through the ages.

Hear Mary, Elizabeth and Israel singing the Magnificat in beautiful harmony. The hymn belongs to all three. The Visitation celebrates the women of the Old Testament longing for a child and the woman of the New Testament who is bearing the child of God.

The Magnificat

My soul magnifies the Lord

And my spirit rejoices in God my Saviour;

Because He has regarded the lowliness of His handmaid;

For behold, henceforth all generations shall call me blessed;

Because He who is mighty has done great things for me,

and holy is His name;

And His mercy is from generation to generation

on those who fear Him.

He has shown might with His arm,

He has scattered the proud in the conceit of their heart.

He has put down the mighty from their thrones,

and has exalted the lowly.

He has filled the hungry with good things,

and the rich He has sent away empty.

He has given help to Israel, his servant, mindful of His mercy

Even as he spoke to our fathers, to Abraham and to his posterity forever.

Luke 1:46-55

GETTING BEYOND

I used to enjoy hearing my aunts and uncles talking about things "getting beyond". It seemed to be a family phrase, and was useful in various circumstances. The two I remember best were Christmas and birthdays for an ever-increasing number of nieces and nephews and the gifts that had to be bought, and any increase in price of anything - bus fares, shop prices, taxes, etc.

One uncle always measured prices and their increase in pounds, shillings and pence (£.s.d.), which made them more dramatic. "Only 50 pence" someone would say. "What!" he would exclaim, "another ten shillings!" But for all their "gettings beyond" they never did stop buying for the children, and then for the following generation. "This will have to stop," they would say, but it never did.

And after Christmas they would agree that it had cost too much, that children had it too easy these days, that they didn't appreciate things as *they* used to when *they* were small, and that Christmas had now become too commercialised. I've heard that all my life, since I was a small boy, so I wonder when it wasn't commercialised. Sometimes I would say so, and receive an answer like "Yes, but it wasn't as bad then as it is now," and I heard that over the years, too. Christmas always was better in the past ... and we can keep on going back to the first one ...

The birth of Jesus at Bethlehem was celebrated by Mary and Joseph and the family who would have been with them at the birth. Every family knows something of that time. We remember that at Christmas. We know what Mary knew and had shared with Joseph, but that no-one would understand - that this child was sent from God to be Messiah and Saviour. So our celebration is richer in family love and faith than the family of Joseph and Mary could have been aware of. Down the centuries we have celebrated that Christ was born for us.

Then, after Christmas, we grumble because we have spent too much, that we have to buy too many presents, that we get sick with too much food and drink and even have to throw a lot of food away, and so many people who are starving and would love to have this food . . . a chorus of discontent that overlies every Christmas that I have known.

Next year, don't grumble. Buy presents willingly or not at all. Choose thoughtfully and not extravagantly, unafraid of what people might think or say about how much or how little you spent. How do you know what they will say? or think? Is it because you think that way yourself, and imagine they would? . . .

Jesus is born for us. We pray and sing carols and celebrate. No grumbles.

"I bring you news of great joy.
A babe has been born for you at Bethlehem"
And a host of the heavenly angels sang
"Glory to God in the highest"

OUR LADY IN ART

Would you easily remember your favourite picture of Our Lady? I have two – amongst many that I love. One is of the young woman standing in a field, lost in a dream of what she has been invited to share; and the other is one of the Annunciation when she first knew of God's love and choice of her.

Of the Annunciation there are many beautifully imagined scenes. Through the ages that moment has been a favourite of artists: the stillness, the drama, the realisation, the acceptance – and the virgin conception has occurred in the overshadowing of the Holy Spirit, the cloud of the presence of God. Every book of Christian painting will have images of the Annunciation.

But of the girl alone I have seen only a couple. How does an artist choose a moment in the nine months? We wonder at the ordinary and everyday that Mary had to live, her secret shared only with Joseph, at first, and then partly with family from the security of Joseph's home (St. Matthew tells the story discreetly and delicately).

We are all familiar with the Christmas crib scene in paintings and in sculpture, but only now and then are the people, mentioned by St Luke as being with Mary and Joseph, ever portrayed – the people who are astounded by what the shepherds had to say. Usually the focus is on the three of the holy family, and the tranquillity suggests there has been a virgin birth to complement the virginal conception. Yet now and then art depicts a resting Mary, the baby is not in her arms and around her are the women who assisted at the birth. We gaze, wanting to know better the moment the artist chose . . .

The greatest number of images of Mary is of the beautiful girl holding her baby – the Madonna and child is said to be the most frequent subject in Christian art. We understand the appeal: the lovely girl has become a mother, the fullness of motherhood gracing the daughter and wife she had been in family. Now she is mother of a new family and home. Every home has known the miracle, every artist been a child held by the mother, but at the centre of the story of birth in our world is the

Incarnation – the Word made flesh, the divine become human: the miracle of life that every child shared made manifest in the birth and life of the Word from whom all creation has being.

We marvel at the beauty and variety of the simple two figures. Study the look on the face of Mary in each such painting that you know. How often she is not gazing at her child, so many times she is looking into a middle distance as though contemplating the mystery she has been asked to share, foreseeing its fullness of suffering that Simeon tells her of at the Presentation, wondering how much of human knowledge she will need to impart to her divine son.

Then there are the moments from Scripture when Mary is in motion – the journey to Bethlehem, the flight into Egypt, the wedding feast at Cana, along the road to Calvary. She is still at the Crucifixion and when she holds the body of Jesus after he is taken down from the cross – and yet watch the motion of the Pieta, Michelangelo's masterpiece, as Mary settles her son's body across her lap. The arms want to hold her son as when he was a boy, but the dead weight is too heavy, so she rests her right arm around his back and waits to see where she will place her left arm when his body is settled. The arm waits in a praying gesture as Jesus' left leg moves to rest alongside the right. Will she cradle him when he is finally still? The Pieta is the most loved sculpture in the history of Christian art, the beautiful final image of the Madonna and child.

Mary is mentioned five times in Matthew's Gospel, only once in Mark and just twice in John's – which is remarkable. At the Crucifixion Jesus gave Mary into John's care "Behold your son . . . behold your mother" and yet John chose only two moments to mention her in the Gospel – at the wedding feast at Cana and at Calvary. Each time she is called "Woman" by Jesus (a most beautiful name) and the sacraments of Baptism and Eucharist are symbolised in water and wine, blood and water. We realise the two stories reflect the same truths.

It is in Luke that we have the best-known references to Our Lady, but in a strange way. In the body of the Gospel and in the Acts of the Apostles (which Luke also wrote) Mary is mentioned only once in each: but in the Nativity stories in chapters one and two she is mentioned frequently. Then we discover that Luke borrowed his opening two chapters to make them his own: it is the original author, not Luke, who so vividly pictures Mary.

What scenes he had presented for Christian art!

The above sketch is taken from a favourite picture of Mary and Jesus. The "Madonnina" (Little Madonna), commonly known as the "Madonna of the Streets", was painted by Roberto Ferruzzi (1854-1934) and first publicly exhibited in 1897 at an art exhibition in Venice. Research says that this was not originally painted as a religious picture, but it has become popular as an image of the Virgin Mary holding her infant son, and is one of the most renowned of Ferruzzi's works. Although the original is said to have disappeared, it has not prevented the great popularity and usage of the image. Copies of the original are frequently featured on prayer cards, portraits and greeting cards.

Mary's Lullaby

Bethlehem

Sleep, my baby, sleep, my child.
Angels are singing, shepherds adore.
My joy I share, the world is redeemed.
Sleep, my babe, now sleep.

Jerusalem

Sleep, my baby, sleep, my child.
Simeon held you, Anna proclaimed:
The joy of your people and light of the world.
Sleep, my babe, now sleep.

Finding in the Temple

Sleep, my son, now sleep, my child.
We sought you in sorrow till the third day.
Your Father's work must now be your way.
Sleep, my child, His Son.

Jesus' Ministry

Break, my heart, pierced with love.
Jesus is gone . . . God's will be done.
My son is God's Word, the seed that must die.
Break, my heart, with love.

Pietà

Sleep, my son, my babe, my child.
Death now holds you, still, my love.
My soul glorifies the living Lord.
Sleep, my son, His Child.

Magnificat : Annunciation

Gifts, my God, you give unto me:
Life and your love and Word of my flesh.
The world will receive, and bless You in me.
Rest, my heart, in peace.

CHRISTMAS IN JANUARY

How soon do you start looking forward to Christmas? One man I know starts in January, at the January sales. He buys all his presents for the following Christmas at the bargain sale prices, and is thus free to give his full spiritual attention to the wonderful celebration of the coming of Christ into our world when December comes.

You and I could do that. Would that ease these December days for you, that you knew all your gifts were bought and wrapped? You would not need to criticise the commercialisation of Christmas if you were not part of it: but then we remember that we are only a part of the commercialisation if we want to be.

Since I was young I have heard people grumble about Christmas, and it has always puzzled me. I found it exciting and fun when I was young, and a glorious spiritual celebration full of thanksgiving to God when its full meaning became clear.

My lovely home always gave me the spiritual, but I needed to grow into its fullness. Now I am enjoying everything about this time - church, family, friends, the sense of sharing something wonderful with the whole Christian world, together with a longing to share that with everyone and the sadness that I do not know how to.

If I see you and wish you a happy Christmas I shall mean what I have just written; that love of Christ be in your heart, and joy with family and friends be yours. I guess you mean the same when you give the greeting - what else can it mean? See you at the January sales!

MY FRIEND MARY

My friend, Mary, died just before Christmas. We had spoken on the phone a little while before. She knew she had not long to live, but she was at peace. She was at her daughter's house, and her room was downstairs next to the kitchen, her bedroom.

She knew how much she was loved. Eileen and Gary wanted her at home with them and she was at peace, her lovely quiet life coming to its close.

It took me back twenty years. Mary had then been looking after her own mother, and also her husband, Gerry. He was dying of cancer and I was with him for Holy Communion and anointing, and he told me what a wonderful wife and mother Mary had been - and what a wonderful daughter to her mother. I had seen it. I knew.

Her mother lived in a tiny terraced house, but wanted to stay there rather than go to Mary's home or any other of the family homes. They understood. But how they loved her and looked after her. Every day they would be in, get the shopping, chat with her.

Mary was with her mother when she was dying. She sat at the end of the bed, looking at her lovely mother - eighty-five years old. She knew she was ready to die, frail and weak at the end of a beautiful quiet life.

Suddenly her mother opened her eyes. She looked straight past Mary and she smiled. She stretched out her arms and said "Oh, you are beautiful!" and then relaxed again and closed her eyes. Those were her last words.

Mary told me of this strange moment. Had her mother seen a vision of Our Lady in that last moment (she loved Our Lady, prayed the Rosary each day)? She longed to think so, but was afraid to tell anyone for fear they would not understand.

Now Mary was dying, looked after by her daughter as beautifully as she had looked after her own mother. The love travels on through a family, doesn't it, and I hope you have seen it in your own home. Children learn love by what they see and understand.

I feel sad when I see the elderly abandoned by their children, safely

27

put out of the way, hardly visited. And I know the same will happen to these children when they become elderly parents. Children live what they learn. Selfish children become lonely parents.

Mary was a beautiful woman - daughter, wife, mother, friend. Now she is with God.

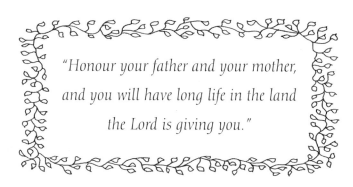

"Honour your father and your mother, and you will have long life in the land the Lord is giving you."

"Our Lady of the Snows"
Santa Maria Maggiore (St Mary Majors) is one of the four Patriarchal Basilicas of Rome.

OUR LADY OF THE SNOWS

When my friend, Father Hugh, retired from the active priestly ministry he decided the first months would be a quiet time of prayer and study – a wonderful start to retirement years! He would spend some of that time in Rome, and set himself a project. He had heard that of the nearly five hundred churches in Rome more than 130 of them were dedicated to Our Lady: so would explore the city, visiting each Marian church.

He never made it. He started enthusiastically, but came to decide that honouring Our Lady was more important than counting her churches. Churches are for prayer and not for a little showing off or boasting. Exploring the city, but without pressure, he made regular visits to his favourite churches of which a number were dedicated to Mary.

His favourite was St. Mary Majors. It is beautiful. Its simple structure recalls the magnificence of Ancient Rome's basilicas – rows of classically proportioned and spaced pillars, the beautiful Cosmatesque floor, the gold decorated ceiling, the fascinating mosaics. It is probably the most beautiful church in the city. Some scholars used to believe it had been a Roman basilica transformed into a Christian church but came to establish that it had been carefully reordered in the 18th century to reflect the perfect proportions of classical Roman architecture.

Other scholars wondered about the legend associated with the title "Our Lady of the Snows", a feast celebrated by the Church on the 5th August. The story tells that a senator, John, wanted to leave his wealth to build a church in honour of Our Lady. In a dream she told him she accepted his wish and there would be a fall of snow (in Roman August!) at the place she wished the church to be built.

The following day Senator John and Pope Liberius – who had had a similar dream – met on the Esquiline Hill, one of the original Seven Hills of Rome, and there was the snow! In the beautiful Borghese Chapel is a relief illustrating the legend and each year, on the feast day, a shower of white petals flutters down from the small dome of this chapel, a tradition which recalls the story.

But was there a church of Our Lady of the Snows here? At the beginning of the 20th century every part of the lovely church was examined and evidence only was found of this 5th century basilica, built following the declaration of the Council of Ephesus in AD341 that gave Mary the title "Theotokos", Mother of God. Scholars were satisfied the story of Our Lady of the Snows was simply a story.

However, there was a startling find. Thousands of bones were buried underneath the basilica in a large mass grave. Only criminals and slaves were buried like this, and they realised that many Christians might have been buried here because a known place for their public execution was at the bottom of the hill. Many condemned criminals would have been executed there and their bones thrown into the Esquiline charnel.

A few years later came a startling surprise. The mosaics of the Old and New Testament along the nave of the church were taken down for cleaning and restoration. They seemed older than the magnificent mosaics of the arch over the Papal Altar and the impression was confirmed by markings on the back of the mosaics: they had clearly been attached to other walls before being incorporated into the present basilica. But where? There is no trace of a church that held these mosaics – so where have they come from. The tantalising answer is: from a fourth century church on this same site, which brings us again to the legend of Our Lady of the Snows! Is there any substance to the legend?

We don't know. Father Hugh smiled as he finished the story of his favourite church: beautiful 5th century basilica, legend of the Snows, beautiful mosaics, Cosmatesque floor (various coloured marble designs), but one shadow – the ceiling decorated with Spanish gold, recalling the horrifying days of Spanish and Portuguese enslavement of the native peoples of Central and South America. Such decoration saddens us but will remain part of the story of Rome's loveliest church in honour of Mary.

HALF A CROWN

When I was nine my parents said we were going to have another baby. We didn't need one, I said – the house was comfortable with four of us. They told me God was giving them another child and they were happy and they wanted me to be, too. I thought about it and decided if it was a boy I'd be pleased.

But it was a girl. I showed my disappointment when my father came to tell us. She is beautiful, he said. You will love her. I didn't know. All the family were there – aunts, uncles, cousins, friends – and they were giving the baby small gifts. I had my half-crown pocket money in my pocket and I carefully placed it in her hand. I remember uncurling her fingers so that I could close them again over the half-crown.

We never saw that half-crown again. She said she didn't ever remember seeing it. You must have spent it, I'd say, and she'd say she must have been robbed. Over the years it became a joke with us. That half-crown had surprising adventures. We accused our parents of using it to pay for a weekend break, having a party at our expense, putting it on a horse and winning a vast fortune which they had stashed away for a ripe old age. Family nonsense that many of you will know when you know that the dafter you think the more fun it becomes.

That half-crown stayed alive over the years, but not now. My sister, Frances, is dead. She was taken by cancer in just six weeks. We saw her fade away from us day after day and then on Christmas Day 2000 she died. I was all morning at the church and then went to the family home for the rest of the day. We took it in turns to be with her and she died at 9.30 that Christmas evening. That was some years ago now, and I'll never be able to smile at the memory of that half-crown. I just see the little fingers as I uncurl them and place the big coin in the tiny hand.

So many happy memories I carry of her. We were so close over the years – part of a large family, sharing many friends, loving our faith in God that meant so much to both of us, and yet tiny memories like this one of the half-crown are part of the whole pattern. Great love has space for tiny memories, and makes them precious.

CHRIST IN XMAS

Do like our Christmas stamp on the back cover of this book? You will understand why we designed it. We who believe want to keep Christ in Christmas. Many dislike "Xmas" as seeming a way of avoiding Christ's name. So, we thought that by putting the Christchild in the manger of the Xmas we would put Christ back into Christmas and change Xmas for everybody who saw and understood.

A friend tells me that when he first saw our Christmas label on his envelope his hackles rose because he so dislikes "Xmas" - but then he laughed when he saw the baby in the X and he realised we had changed Xmas to the babe's manger: Christ was in Xmas.

Many have told us how attractive they find the stamp and its gently-worded Christmas blessing. We plan to have the stamps always available for those who ask - as a sign of faith in the Incarnation, as a friendly greeting in our Christian way and as a way of reminding us that faith in Christ is the inspiration of our Christmas rejoicing. I can now wish you "Happy Xmas" and you know exactly what I mean.

I wish I knew the man who celebrates Christmas every day, but I only know about him. Every day he has Christmas dinner, every evening wraps his presents and every morning opens them. I would willingly wish him Happy Christmas every day - which, we might say, is what we do when we pray for family and friends in our daily prayer.

May the peace of Christ be yours in the love of each day.